This Book has been officially
discarded by Princeton Elementary
Schools District 115

DISNEY'S WORLD OF ADVENTURE

THE OUTDOOR

CONTENTS

Swiss Family Robinson   7
Backpacking—The Easy Way   36
Big Bird   42
Mickey and Goofy On a Wilderness Trek   47
Malay Pirates   55
Getting "Unlost"   58

Photograph Credits:
CYR Color Photo Agency, 46; A. Devaney, Inc., 42 both, 44, 45; Joseph Popp/Anthro-Photo, 43.

Copyright © 1977 by Walt Disney Productions.

All rights reserved under International and Pan-American Copyright Conventions. Published in the United States by Random House, Inc., New York, and simultaneously in Canada by Random House of Canada Limited, Toronto.

Library of Congress Cataloging in Publication Data

Disney (Walt) Productions. Disney's world of adventure presents The outdoor adventure book. contents: Swiss family Robinson.—Backpacking—the easy way.—Big bird. [etc.] 1. Camping. 2. Backpacking. [1. Family life—Fiction. 2. Survival—Fiction. 3. Camping. 4. Backpacking] I. Title. PZ7.D6250u 1977 [Fic] 77-74468 ISBN 0-394-83601-4   ISBN 0-394-93601-9 lib. bdg.

Manufactured in the United States of America
1 2 3 4 5 6 7 8 9 0

presents

ADVENTURE BOOK

Random House 🏠 New York

Swiss Family Robinson

Shipwrecked

Halfway through the storm, the ship's mainmast broke. It crashed through the deck and trapped the Swiss family Robinson in their cabin.

The five of them and all they owned in the world were in the tiny cabin. They'd been living in it for weeks, on their way to New Guinea. None of them wanted to die in it.

The mast had crashed through the cabin's ceiling, landing right in front of the door. Johann, the father of the Robinson family, stared at the blocked door with horror. He yelled for help from his eldest son, Fritz, a sturdy, red-headed boy of sixteen. Together they tried to pull the door open. But it gave only a few inches. Every time the ship rolled, water poured in on them.

Ernst, the Robinsons' dark-haired middle son, was fourteen and much thinner than his brother. He managed to squeeze partway through the narrow opening. "Help us, somebody!" he shouted. "Get us out of here!"

No one answered. Earlier in the evening, the ship had sailed into the storm in an effort to escape pirates. The Robinson family had been sent to their cabin, and had heard nothing from the crew since then.

Johann's wife, Elizabeth, huddled on a bunk with their youngest son, eight-year-old Francis. It didn't seem fair, she thought. They'd come all the way from Europe and were almost to New Guinea when the pirate ships were sighted. She prayed they'd get out alive.

Johann pulled Ernst back in. He was soaked. Water kept sloshing into the cabin. In the hold below, the cargo of farm animals began to bawl as they got wetter and wetter.

Suddenly, over the storm's noise came a dreadful, ear-splitting crash. The ship tilted sharply to one side. Luggage flew across the cabin. Flaming oil from the lantern hit the wet floor and burned briefly in puddles.

"Lord have mercy on us!" cried Elizabeth.

"And the animals too, Lord," whispered Francis. The pitiful cries of the animals upset him more than anything.

The ship had now stopped moving, but huge waves still crashed against it. Johann was afraid it would sink. "Smash the bunks and use them to break open the door!" he ordered. "We must get out before she goes down!"

By the time the Robinsons freed themselves, it was morning and the storm was over. Blue sky and sunshine greeted them as they climbed onto the deck. The ship, they discovered, was stuck on rocks not far from land.

"Captain Wilhelm?" Johann called. "Captain Wilhelm!"

"Hello, there!" yelled Fritz. "Anyone around?"

"If the crew were still on board, they'd have heard us long before now," Elizabeth said. "But I can't believe they'd just go off and—"

"Did the pirates get them, Father?" Francis asked.

"I don't know, son. I'm just grateful that *our* lives were spared."

"Oh, Johann," Elizabeth wept. "What will we do now? All our hopes wrecked, our dreams of a better life in New Guinea—"

"Don't cry, Mother," said Ernst. "Maybe I could swim to land and get help to repair the ship."

His older brother looked doubtfully at the bare rocks and the tree-lined beach ahead of them. To the left of the beach was a high cliff. To the right and beyond lay miles of jungle. There were no signs of life anywhere. "It's probably a deserted island," Fritz said. "But I think we should build a raft and get to shore. This ship could sink any minute!"

Johann figured the ship wouldn't sink right away, since it was holding fast on the rocks. But at sea anything might happen, he thought. "Let's find saws and hammers and get to work," he said grimly. "We only have a few hours. If we try to leave after the tide turns, we'll drift out to sea."

The Robinson family was good at inventing things. By afternoon they had built an odd-looking raft from boards and halves of barrels. Five of the barrels were for the family to sit in. The rest were for food and equipment. The sailing ship was carrying not only animals but

8

tools, seeds, and other farming supplies. And there were telescopes and compasses in the captain's cabin. The Robinsons decided to take as much of this gear as they could. They had no idea how long they might wait to be rescued.

After they lowered the raft into the water, they lashed on oars and a rudder. Johann looked the raft over. "Well, it's a strange craft. We'll need to take along bailing buckets," he said. "But we've done our best. Let's pack the supplies and go."

Suddenly Francis came flying out of the hold, followed by two huge dogs. "What about Turk and Flora?" he called. "We can't leave them behind!"

Like everyone else, Johann felt sorry for the animals. But he knew his family came first. "When all the Robinsons are safe on land, then you may talk to me about animals," he said. "Not before."

"But, Father—"

"Francis, stop asking!" Johann roared. "If we took them we'd sink for sure!"

So they left the dogs. One after the other, each member of the family swung by a rope onto the raft. They were quite a sight, sitting in their little tubs among bags of grain, muskets, shovels, and rakes. Ernst, who liked to read, had lined the bottom of his barrel with books. Fritz had slipped a few extra tools into his tub. Elizabeth held her sewing bag in one hand and gripped Francis's arm with the other. Knowing Francis, she was afraid that he'd swim back for the dogs.

At the last minute, Johann found room for a few chickens. Then the family cast off. Fritz and Ernst each manned an oar. Johann steered with the rudder. It was hard rowing through the high waves. But slowly the ship was left behind.

Along the empty deck the dogs ran back and forth, howling. Francis couldn't stand it. When no one was looking, he waved to them. They jumped over the side. "Here come the dogs," he said to his father. "I guess they're going to swim."

His two older brothers grinned at each other. "Wonder who called them?" Ernst said.

"I can't imagine!" said Fritz.

After swimming awhile, the dogs caught up with the raft. But they were too tired to keep going. They tried to climb aboard, and water

9

sloshed into the barrels. Johann didn't have the heart to push the dogs back into the sea. "Stop rowing and start bailing!" he shouted.

Bailing hard, the family somehow managed to stay afloat, even with the dogs. Elizabeth petted Flora. She had to admit she felt safer with the dogs along. "You see, Johann, they didn't sink us," she said.

"So I see," Johann said with a smile. "But we'd better get to shore. One miracle a day is all we can hope for!"

The raft finally reached land. The Robinsons were all thankful to be safe. But they were also a little afraid of what they might find ashore. The beach was beautiful, with sparkling white sand and a border of waving palm trees. Coconuts hung from the palms like beads. Flocks of colorful birds dove for fish along the shore. Well, fish and coconuts make good food, Johann thought. But who else lives here in the dense jungle, behind the border of palms? Or is this place, as Fritz said, a deserted island? Johann couldn't tell.

For now, the beach seemed the safest place to stay. The Robinsons dragged their raft ashore and unloaded it. By sundown they had made a tent of driftwood poles and sails, and were ready to camp for the night.

As the sky darkened, they gathered around a fire. Elizabeth served a soup that she'd made with food from the ship. Their soup bowls were coconut shells, which Francis had found on the beach. As they ate, animals cried and birds called through the jungle behind them. They found the place pleasant and scary at the same time.

"How long do you think we'll have to stay here?" Elizabeth asked.

Johann shrugged. "I don't know. If no one lives here, there's no one to help rebuild the ship." He sighed. "Of course, I don't even know if it can be rebuilt at all." He shook his head sadly. "I'm sorry we ever left Switzerland."

"Don't say that, Father." Fritz set down his soup bowl. "If we'd stayed, both Ernst and I would already be fighting in Napoleon's war."

Ernst nodded. "Even if the ship did get wrecked, Father, we were right to try for a new life somewhere else."

"And there are animals here, too," said Francis sleepily. "I bet I could start my own zoo."

Everyone laughed. "Just be careful, young man," said his mother. "We know you like animals, but there may be some that don't like *you!*"

A Home in the Jungle

The next morning, the ship was still on the rocks. Johann decided they should rescue more of the cargo. He especially wanted to get all the animals still trapped in the hold. He, Ernst, and Fritz climbed back into the raft and rowed away.

Left on the shore with Francis, Elizabeth began to mend a rip in the tent. Halfway through she ran out of thread. "Francis," she said, "would you get me some thread from my bag?" When no one answered, she looked up. She was alone. "Francis? Francis, where are you?" she called. "Francis, come here!"

There were no sounds except the pounding surf and the sigh of the wind in the palm trees. Frightened, Elizabeth called the dogs. Holding their collars, she walked past the palms and slowly entered the jungle. Huge trees towered over her. "Francis?" she called again. Suddenly Flora and Turk both growled.

"Shh!" came a small voice from somewhere ahead. "Don't scare him off." In the middle of a clearing, Francis was trying to capture a baby elephant. He had a stalk of sugar cane in one hand and the end of a rope snare in the other. "Here, little elephant," he called softly. "Come on, fella, I won't hurt you."

The elephant was not so easily fooled. It moved around nervously —but came closer and closer to the loop of rope on the ground. At last it stepped into the snare. Francis quickly pulled the rope tight around the elephant's foot and wound the other end around a tree trunk. "Gotcha!" he said happily. The baby elephant lifted its trunk and trumpeted in distress.

A sudden sound behind Francis made him turn around. With a low roar, a tiger sprang out of the trees. It had heard the elephant's cries. "Get away!" Francis yelled. "This one's mine!"

Elizabeth nearly fainted. "Flora! Turk! Go get him!" she shouted. "Francis—stay there and don't move!"

Snarling and barking, the dogs surprised the tiger by attacking from both sides. The big cat fled into the jungle.

"You could have been killed!" Elizabeth said angrily. "Well? Don't you have anything to say?"

Francis hung his head. "I'm sorry I did it but—"

"But what?"

"Can I keep the elephant anyway?"

His mother smiled. It was hard to stay angry at Francis. "I suppose so," she said, ruffling his reddish-blond hair. "But next time—would you please catch something *smaller*?"

By the time Elizabeth and Francis got back to the beach, the rest of the family had returned. They had brought the ducks and more chickens in the barrels of the raft. The cow, pig, goats, and donkey had been tied to the raft with long ropes and made to swim. It was a hard day's work for everyone.

For several more days the Robinsons kept unloading the ship. They also worked on plans to build a tree house. They had discovered a giant tree in the jungle. It was not far from the beach, across a beautiful stream. A tree house, said Johann, would be the safest place to live. It would protect them from tigers and other dangers. Besides, he liked the idea of living high in a tree. So did his sons.

The family first cleared brush away from under the tree. Then they cut down smaller trees and sawed them into planks. They rigged up pulleys to haul the lumber into the big tree. They had never built a house before. It was fun learning how. But Elizabeth could never quite share everyone else's excitement.

"The world is full of plain people who live in plain houses on the ground," Johann said to her one day. "Didn't you ever dream of having a tree house?"

Elizabeth looked annoyed. "Mostly I dreamed of having a house in New Guinea," she said. She stared up at the thick platforms they had built, high in the branches of the tree. "You must think we're going to be here a long time."

"I have no way of knowing, my dear," Johann said. "But we can't spend our days just waiting for a ship to come by."

"Couldn't we light a signal fire though—just in case one comes?"

"What if the pirates were to see it?" Fritz said. "Right now being alive is more important than being found."

Elizabeth sighed and looked up into the tree again, just in time to see Francis climbing a rope ladder to the highest platform. She was horrified. "Francis, come down here!" she ordered.

"Aw, please—can't I stay a little while?"

"Elizabeth, let him be. He'll be all right," said Johann.

"Well, tie a rope around him in case he falls."

After Ernst had tied a rope on Francis, Elizabeth turned away. She couldn't look anymore. She hated the idea of living in the air. Like in a bird's nest, she thought. She felt sure the tree house would be uncomfortable and unsafe.

Francis kept climbing higher in the tree. He had spotted a baby monkey. "Here, little monkey," he called. "C'mere—I won't hurt you." He inched forward onto one of the pulley lines.

Ernst saw him first. "Francis, what are you trying to do?" he yelled. "Francis—look out!"

But it was too late. Francis fell. Held by the rope around his waist,

he swung back and forth in the air. When he got over being afraid, he began giggling. Everyone looked so funny upside down!

His brother rushed to rescue him. Elizabeth said angrily, "Suppose I hadn't just *happened* to insist that he wear that rope?"

"I know you're upset," Johann said, "but try to understand—"

"You do what you want about this place," Elizabeth snapped. "Just keep Francis on the ground and leave me out of it!" Without another word she turned and walked away.

The boys waited for their father to answer. "All right, we'll do that," Johann called after her. "You stay at the beach camp until everything's fixed up—and *then* we'll see how you feel!"

After Elizabeth left, the others worked even harder. Francis trained his elephant to help, which made the hauling easy. They made many more trips to the ship. Luckily, it showed no sign of sinking. They brought back barrels of nails, dishes, even furniture.

The house took several months to finish. During all this time Elizabeth stayed in the beach camp. She taught herself how to cook the different fish that the boys caught. She found wild greens in the nearby jungle. She also cared for and fed all the animals, which were kept tied until there would be time to build pens. Elizabeth felt lonely and left out. But she didn't go anywhere near the tree house.

Then one evening Johann told her the house was finished. The next morning he and the boys took her to see it.

"You're going to be surprised," Ernst said proudly. In fact, he was surprised himself. Ernst hadn't really been sure that they could build a house—or that he would be much help. Unlike Fritz, who could do anything with a hammer, Ernst was usually all thumbs. But he had learned to be a good carpenter, though he still liked books better than beams.

When Elizabeth reached the clearing around the giant tree, she stopped and gasped. The crude, open platforms in the tree were gone. In their place were three pretty thatched huts set high in the branches. The lowest hut had a front porch with a railing around it.

"I can't believe it!" said Elizabeth. "I never dreamed the tree house would look like this!"

"You haven't seen anything yet!" said Fritz, grinning. He took her arm and led her forward. The stream in the clearing was now spanned by a bridge. Guiding his mother across it, Fritz pointed out the guardrails. "You won't even fall off this!" he teased.

As they neared the giant tree, Elizabeth got another surprise. At the base of the tree, Johann and the boys had built a kitchen. It had a sink, a cooler, a clay stove, a table, and barrels to store things in.

"How did you ever do it?" asked Elizabeth.

"Well, the sink's really a turtle shell," Francis said.

Ernst pointed to some pipes. "They're split bamboo. Water from the stream goes over a wheel and into the pipes and then into this barrel—"

"And then right into the sink," finished Fritz, as he opened the tap at the bottom of the barrel. "See? Running water—the latest thing in kitchens!"

"It was Ernst's idea and Fritz built it," Johann said. "And now we'll show you the upstairs. First stop—living room!"

He led the way up a steep staircase, through a trap door, and into

a lovely room. It held furniture from the captain's cabin on the ship. Pots of colorful flowers hung from the roof beams. Along one wall, narrow shelves held pretty dishes. From the front porch, Elizabeth had a fine view of the jungle.

Johann went to a ship's wheel mounted near the stairway railing. "Watch this," he said. He turned the wheel. The bottom part of the staircase rose slowly from the ground. "You can pull up your stairs at night to keep out nosy neighbors," he said, laughing.

Johann showed her the stairs that went up to the boys' room. Then he led her carefully up a stairway off the other side of the living room. "Madame," he said, bowing. "Your room."

Elizabeth gazed at the hand-painted bed, the spinning wheel, the cracked but carefully hung mirror. The house was so beautiful—and so safe. It had strong walls like a regular house and guardrails all over. She felt ashamed that she had been against the tree house. "What's this?" she asked softly, pulling on a thick rope that hung over the bed. "Is it to ring for the butler?"

Johann laughed. "That's the best part." He pulled the rope hand over hand. A section of the roof opened above the bed. "Remember how you once wanted to sleep under the stars? Look up now," he said.

Elizabeth looked through the opened roof at the top of the tree and the clear blue sky. She smiled. "I'm sure there aren't any roofs that open like this in New Guinea."

One by one the boys climbed the stairs to join their parents. "Do you like it?" they asked Elizabeth.

"Everything except the curtains," she said with a sly grin.

"Oh, don't worry about those," Johann said, teasing. "We know a woman who can fix anything!"

Elizabeth looked at them all fondly. Their worn clothing was full of holes. "I think that woman's first job," she said, "will be to make those curtains into clothes!"

Danger on the Coast

After the tree house was finished, the Robinsons had time to explore the land around them. Ernst and Fritz made a dugout boat. They were eager to sail along the coast, to see if they were on an island or just a peninsula. Also, they thought they might find other people somewhere. Elizabeth felt the boys ought to go, but Johann wouldn't hear of it. He no longer wanted to be rescued. He didn't want to give up the tree house, the animal pens he was making, the garden the family had put in. Johann was perfectly happy where he was. To keep the boys busy, he had them make a study of the different plants and animals in the jungle.

"These are all the animals we've seen so far," Ernst said one morning, handing his father a list.

Johann looked up from his workbench near the tree house. "Hmmn, let's see," he said. "Tiger, bear, elephant, hyena, turtle, manatee, monkey, lizard—"

"HELP—SOMEBODY—QUICK!"

It was Francis yelling, somewhere nearby. Johann dropped the list and ran with Ernst across the clearing. Behind them came Flora and Turk, barking madly. At the edge of the jungle a squawking ostrich burst out of a clump of bushes. It had a rope around one foot. At the other end of the rope was Francis, being dragged along.

"Let go, Francis!" Johann shouted.

"I can't! He'd get away!"

Johann and Ernst grabbed the rope but couldn't hold the big bird still. Flora and Turk kept running around, nipping at its feet. Then Fritz arrived with a coat, which he tied over the bird's head. The ostrich bounced around angrily while everyone hung on, red-faced and laughing.

"Good catch!" Elizabeth called to Francis from the kitchen. "Now Ernst can add 'ostrich' to his list."

"And we can ride him!" said Fritz.

Francis was delighted. "Ride him? Let me try! Help me up, somebody!"

"I think you'd better wait until we train him a little," Johann gasped, still laughing. "There's no telling *where* he'd take you today!"

Soon the ostrich was calm enough so that the boys could handle it alone. Johann sat down beside Elizabeth to catch his breath. He stared thoughtfully at his sons. "Don't you sometimes feel that this is the kind of life we were meant to live?" he asked her. "Everything we need seems to be right here at our fingertips."

Elizabeth shook her head. "Not *everything*," she said.

"What do you mean?"

She looked around at the house and garden, the neat animal pens, the land that had been so hard to clear. "All this is fine for today," she said. "But what about tomorrow? What future is there here for our sons?"

Johann looked uncomfortable. This was something he hated talking about.

"Suppose we never get away from here? Suppose the boys never have a chance to get married?"

Johann sighed. "Well, what do you suggest?"

"I think we'd better let Fritz and Ernst sail along the coast," Elizabeth said. "Sooner or later they'll have to try, and it might as well be now."

So after a few days of getting ready, the older boys set out in their sailboat, loaded with food and supplies. They kept close to the coast, as Johann had warned them to do. At first they saw nothing but empty beaches like their own. But on the fifth day, as they sailed around a rocky headland, Fritz suddenly jumped up. "Ernst—what's that ahead—in the next bay? Get the glass!"

Ernst peered through the telescope. "Two ships!" he said. "People moving on shore—I can't tell if there's a village—"

"Let me see." Fritz stared long and hard through the glass. "Looks like pirates to me," he said. "Quick—take down the sail or they'll see us." He turned the rudder so the boat pointed to a gap between some rocks. We'd better get to shore," he said. "They won't see us if we go through here."

"I don't think we can!" Ernst cried. The sea was very rough around the rocks. He tried to row, but he knew they were going wrong. The sea boiled and churned in the narrow gap. Wild currents spun the little boat.

"Watch out!" Fritz yelled. "Bring it around the other way!"

The boys paddled hard, but they couldn't control the boat. They flew high in the air on a mountainous wave. Then they came down on a rock. The boat split open. The boys and all their supplies spilled into the surf.

Fritz and Ernst swam for their lives. Dangerous currents pulled at them, and waves broke over their heads. More than once they were dashed against the rocks. Luckily they weren't far from shore. A large wave finally caught them and threw them onto the beach.

Almost all their supplies were lost. Fritz managed to rescue a bedroll, and Ernst still had the compass tied on a thong around his neck. They stood dripping in their soggy clothes while he checked it. "It still works," Ernst said. "But we don't even have a knife. What are we going to do?"

In vain Fritz searched his pockets. It was true—they had no weapon of any kind.

"Don't worry, little brother, we'll think of something," Fritz said. "But first we'd better see what those pirates are up to."

Ernst looked frightened, but he nodded. The boys made two backpacks from the bedroll, so they could have their hands free. Then they crept carefully along the bay beach to a hiding place behind some rocks. From there they could watch what was going on.

The pirates were farther down the shore, next to several longboats pulled up on the sand. Two groups of men were standing around while their leaders divided a large pile of loot. It was a noisy scene, with rum bottles everywhere, and a lot of arguing back and forth. The pirates wore baggy pants, scarves on their heads, and rings in their ears. They were a mean-looking bunch.

Suddenly Ernst grabbed his brother's arm. "Look over there," he said. "Under the trees." He pointed out two prisoners, tied hand and foot. One was an old man in a sea captain's uniform. The other seemed to be a cabin boy. A little smaller than Ernst, he was dressed in a large cap and ill-fitting sailor's clothes.

While Ernst and Fritz watched, the two pirate leaders came up and grabbed the boy. They seemed about to drag him toward the pile of loot on the beach. Then the old captain said something. After a brief argument with him, the pi-

rates threw the boy down and went back to their men.

"You know," Fritz whispered, "we could sneak in there and free them before the pirates knew what was happening."

"Don't be stupid," said Ernst. "It won't work."

"It's now or never," Fritz whispered. "Come on." He started into the jungle.

Ernst followed, but only because he was afraid to stay alone. Keeping low, the boys circled the bay at the edge of the trees and crept up to the prisoners from behind. "Shh!" Fritz whispered to them. "Don't make a sound.

"Who are you?" whispered the captain, trying to look at Fritz out of the corner of his eye.

"We've come to help," Fritz said. He worked at the old man's ropes, while Ernst pulled at the thongs that bound the boy.

"If we only had a knife," moaned Ernst.

"Don't waste time on me," the captain said. "I'm valuable for ransom and they won't harm me. Get the boy free and go—quickly!"

"But I don't want to leave without you," said the boy.

"No, you must get away if you can," the captain said. "I'll come back for you soon."

Just as Ernst and Fritz got the boy untied, they heard loud shouts from the beach. The two pirate leaders were running toward them, waving knives.

"Hurry!" said the captain. "Run for your lives!"

The Cabin Boy's Trick

Fritz and Ernst rushed headlong into the jungle, dragging the cabin boy with them. The pirates were close behind. The Robinsons were able to run hard, but the younger boy wasn't. He lagged, caught his foot, and then fell. "I can't—it hurts," he panted, holding his side.

Fritz and Ernst pulled him under a bush with big, low leaves. "It's going to hurt a lot more when a knife rips through your side," warned Fritz.

"Please—you go on—I'm sorry," the boy whispered. "I didn't want to come with you anyway."

Ernst and Fritz looked at each other. They didn't know what to do. They could hear the pirates beating the bushes not far away. "We can't leave him, but we can't drag him either. He'd slow us down," Ernst said. "Let's just hope they don't find us right away."

Fritz nodded. "All right, catch your breath," he said to the boy. "But remember, when we say run, you run. What's your name?"

"Bertie." The boy was still holding his side.

"You a cabin boy?"

"Not really," Bertie said. "I was just along on one of my grandfather's ships."

"The old gentleman back there is your grandfather?"

Bertie nodded. Then he studied the two boys, noting their torn, wet clothes made of curtain material. "Who are you?" he asked, suddenly afraid. "How did you get here?"

"Shipwrecked," Ernst whispered. "Our family—" He broke off when Fritz jabbed him in the ribs. A pirate was getting close.

Fritz peeked out and saw one of the pirate leaders coming. "You hit him low and I'll hit him high," he whispered to Ernst.

"What about me?" asked Bertie.

"Run!" Fritz gave him a shove, and the boy stumbled out from under the bush. Shouting, the huge pirate turned to rush after Bertie. But at that instant Fritz crashed into his shoulder and Ernst hit his knees. The pirate fell, dropping his knife. Quickly Fritz grabbed it and swung its heavy handle down on the man's skull. Stunned, the pirate lay still. Ernst bent to remove a pistol from his belt.

"Hurry!" Fritz urged. "The others are coming!"

Ernst gave one last tug and the pistol was in his hand. Then he and Fritz ran after Bertie.

By running and resting, running and resting, they managed to hide from the pirates all afternoon. Toward evening they dragged themselves wearily to a high, open hilltop. They looked around. It was quite clear now that they were on a large island. They could see water on the horizon in every direction. On one side the sea was close to them. They could look down into the pirates' bay.

"There they go!" Fritz said. The pirate ships were moving out of the bay.

"It could be a trick to get us to come back," said Ernst.

Fritz thought a minute. "We don't need to go back to the beach at all. We'll cut across the island instead of going back around the coast. It'll be safer and shorter."

"Right," said Ernst, studying the compass. He pointed off across the island. "That's the direction we want—south by southwest."

Fritz nodded. "We can go a little way until dark and then start again at daylight."

"Where are we going?" asked Bertie.

"Home," Ernst said. Without supplies, there was nowhere else they could go.

"But my grandfather will look for me here," Bertie said.

"Don't worry," said Fritz. "You'll be all right. If your grandfather doesn't find you here, he'll sail along the coast—"

"And he couldn't pass our place unseen even if he wanted to," Ernst said, laughing. "Our mother's got an eagle eye for ships!" He shouldered his pack and strode off behind Fritz, leaving Bertie to bring up the rear.

"That's the way, right through there," Ernst said, checking his compass when they came to a narrow river.

Fritz nodded, studying the river. He placed his pack and the captured knife on the ground. Then he began to take off his shirt. "Doesn't look like it'll be over our heads," he said.

"What are you doing?" asked Bertie, who had just arrived.

"Take your clothes off," said Fritz, "and carry them over your head."

Bertie looked shocked.

"It's better than walking for hours in wet clothes," Ernst explained.

"I—I can't swim," Bertie said, backing off.

"You won't have to," Fritz said. "Now come on, it'll be dark soon. Let's get going." He started to take off his pants.

Suddenly Bertie seized the pistol from Ernst's pack. "I'm going back to the beach to wait for my grandfather," he said. "Don't come any closer." He held the gun very steady and aimed it at the two boys.

Fritz and Ernst stared in disbelief. "But that's my pistol!" Ernst cried. Give it back."

"I'm sorry," Bertie said. "I'll see that my grandfather pays you for it." He backed down the trail.

Ernst began to follow but Fritz held him back. "Keep his attention," he whispered. "I'll slip around behind."

Ernst nodded. Quickly he made a slingshot from his compass thong and picked up a stone. Then he walked toward Bertie, who was trying to look in all directions at once. "You'd better drop that pistol," Ernst said, and let his slingshot go. The stone sailed over the boy's head.

Bertie took cover behind a rock. "Don't do that," he begged, as he watched Ernst put another stone in the sling. "I don't want to shoot you, Ernst. Please put it down."

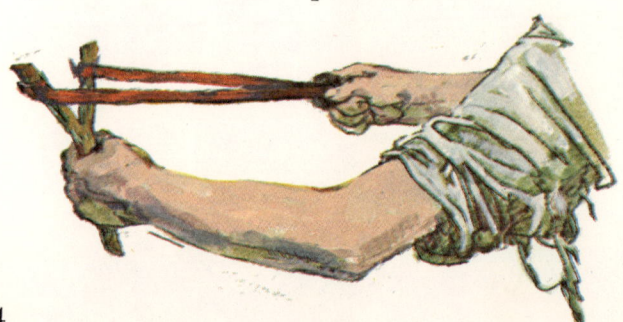

A moment later Fritz reached Bertie from behind. Sneaking up quietly, he tried to seize the pistol. It went off. A bullet hit the dirt between Ernst's feet.

"Why you little—" Furious, Fritz knocked the gun out of Bertie's hand and hurled him to the ground. He was about to punch the boy when suddenly he pulled back.

Ernst came running up. "Let me at him, Fritz," he yelled. "I'll teach him not to shoot at me!"

But Fritz stood up and held Ernst back. "No, it was my fault," he said. "She didn't mean to fire."

"I don't care—I could've been killed!" He suddenly stopped. "Did you say *she*?" Ernst stared at the person now sobbing in front of them.

It was clearly a girl. Her large sailor cap had come off, letting her long, dark, curly hair tumble down.

Surprises for Christmas

Elizabeth sat down to play the organ as Johann had asked. It was Christmas Eve, and time to sing carols. But her heart wasn't in it. Three weeks had passed since Fritz and Ernst left the tree house. She couldn't help thinking that they were hurt or even dead.

Behind her Johann and Francis were singing as loud as they could. Then a key stuck and Elizabeth stopped playing. "Probably got wet on the raft," Johann said.

Elizabeth looked up at him. He hadn't said a word about the boys. She knew he was trying to hide his fears for her sake. "I still don't see how you managed to get this huge organ off the ship by yourself," she said.

Johann said quietly, "Fritz and Ernst helped before they left. It was going to be—well—it's from all of us. Merry Christmas, my dear."

Elizabeth tried to smile. "Thank you," she said, but her eyes were full of tears.

Francis was feeling strange and lonely. He sat down in front of the small Christmas "tree." He and his mother had decorated a bush with shells and berries and all the shiny things they could find. At the top they put a dried starfish, rubbed with pollen to color it gold. Under the tree were several unopened packages, wrapped in leaves and tied with vines. "Suppose Fritz and Ernst don't *ever* come back," said Francis. "What will we do with their presents?"

"Francis, it's very late. Go to bed," Johann said, and gave him a firm push toward the stairs.

Elizabeth sat tight-lipped, trying not to cry. It's all my fault, she said to herself. I was the one who wanted them to go.

"Play something," Johann said. "Play 'Tannenbaum.'"

Elizabeth pumped the foot pedals and then moved her fingers across the organ's yellowed keys. "O Christmas tree," Johann sang, "O Christmas tree . . ."

But Elizabeth just couldn't go on. Sobbing, she put her head down on the keyboard. Johann could think of nothing comforting to say.

Suddenly the dogs, who had been dozing in a corner, both raised their heads at once. Then with a deep growl Turk moved to the stairway and looked down. Flora whined.

"What is it, girl?" asked Johann. He smoothed the ruffled fur on her back. Then he too heard it, though at first he couldn't believe his ears. "O Christmas tree," came the distant voices, "O Christmas tree . . ."

Elizabeth rushed out to the porch and stood clutching the rail. The singing came nearer. By this time Francis had heard it, too. He dashed down from his room, spun the wheel to lower the stairs, and went running toward the sound. He was just past the animal pens when Ernst and Fritz came out of the jungle. They were leading a young zebra on which a girl rode.

Francis came to a full stop. "Where'd you get *that*?" he shouted, pointing at the zebra. "And where'd you get *her*? We though you were dead!"

"Not dead, just a little lost!" yelled Fritz. He grabbed Francis and swung him wildly in the air.

"It's an island, not a peninsula!" Ernst yelled to his parents. "Merry Christmas! Hello! Meet Bertie!"

Talking nonstop, the boys led Bertie into the tree house. Francis made his brothers open their presents right away.

"A new shirt!" Fritz cried. "Just what I needed."

"Me, too," said Ernst, showing off his present. Everyone laughed because it was so true. The shirts they were wearing were in shreds.

"Tell about getting lost," Francis begged.

"Well—" Ernst, beginning the story, told about the wrecked sailboat and the pirates.

"Then after we found out Bertie was really Roberta," Fritz went on, with a grin at the girl, "we tried to cross the river. The first thing that happened was that Ernst went under. When he came up the compass was gone."

"No wonder it took you so long," said Elizabeth. "How did you manage without a compass?"

"We set our course by the sun,"

26

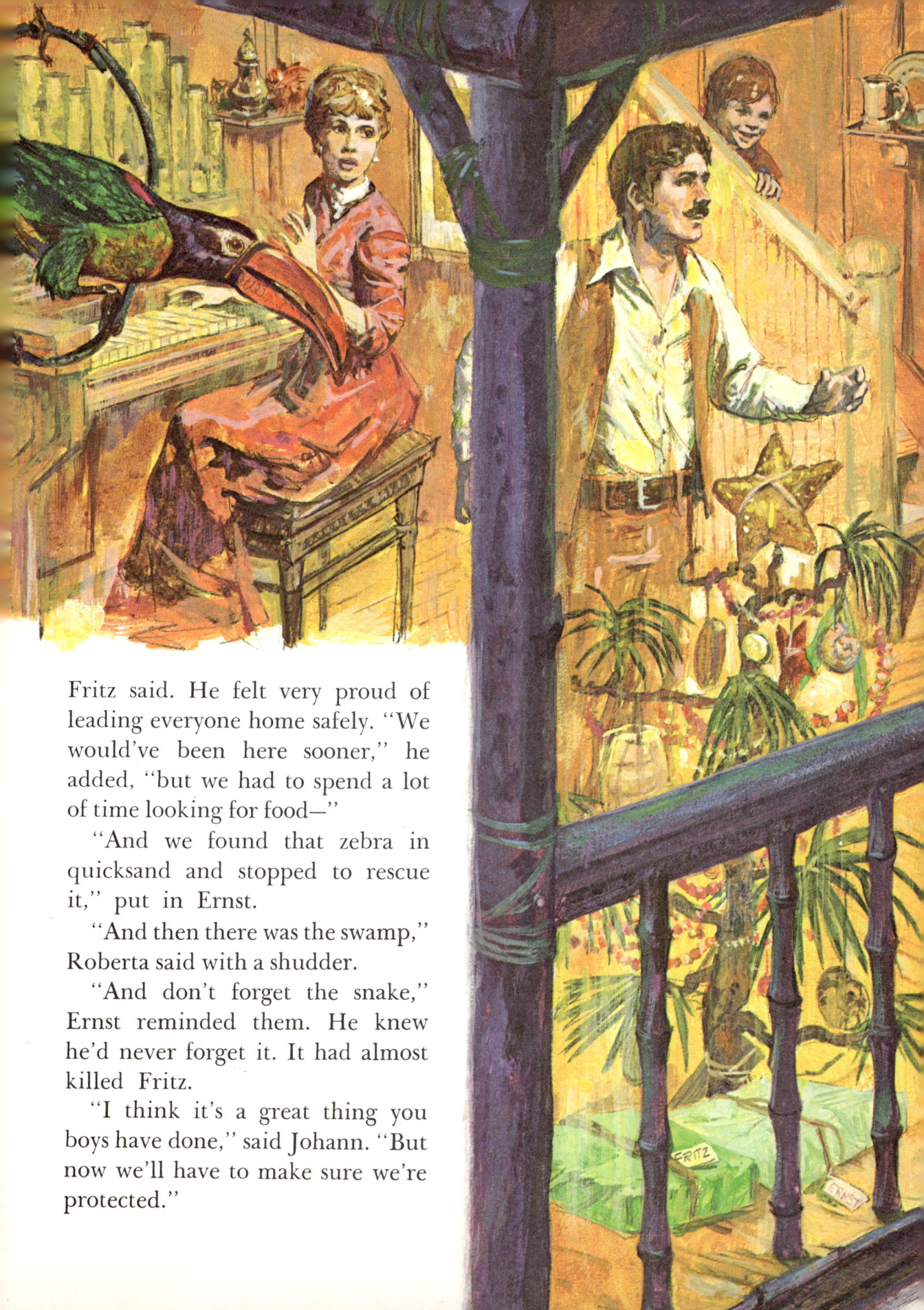

Fritz said. He felt very proud of leading everyone home safely. "We would've been here sooner," he added, "but we had to spend a lot of time looking for food—"

"And we found that zebra in quicksand and stopped to rescue it," put in Ernst.

"And then there was the swamp," Roberta said with a shudder.

"And don't forget the snake," Ernst reminded them. He knew he'd never forget it. It had almost killed Fritz.

"I think it's a great thing you boys have done," said Johann. "But now we'll have to make sure we're protected."

"Father, what do you mean?" Fritz asked.

"Just that the pirates know you're somewhere on this island with one of their prisoners."

"But they think Roberta's just a cabin boy," said Ernst.

Johann shook his head. "They've probably found out by now that Captain Smith's granddaughter was traveling with him. They might think of holding *her* for ransom."

Fritz and Ernst looked uneasy. They hadn't thought of that. Nor had Roberta, who suddenly felt frightened.

"Pirates? I'll shoot 'em," yelled Francis. He pretended to aim a crossbow.

Elizabeth smiled. "I'm afraid it'll take more than bows and arrows to stop pirates," she said.

"What about the cannon?" asked Ernst. "Can't we bring it in from the ship?"

"It's rusted out," said Johann.

"If only we could have gotten it off the ship that day we got the organ," Fritz moaned. They had started to move it but a storm had come up.

"Let's not waste time crying over what couldn't be done," said Johann. "First thing tomorrow morning, we'll go out to the ship. We'll take off everything we can use, and then—" He fell silent.

"And then what, dear?" Elizabeth asked.

"And then blow it up," Johann finished quietly. He knew she'd be upset. She had always hoped that one day they'd rebuild the ship.

"Must you?" Elizabeth asked.

Johann nodded. "Once the pirates see it, they'll be here in a minute," he said. "We need a little time to get ready."

Ready for Pirates

The next morning after breakfast, the family talked about how they could protect themselves from pirates.

"We could have trees bent over and held with snares," Ernst said. "And then when a pirate stepped into the rope circle—whoosh!" He raised his arm to show how the tree would swing the man into the air.

"Well, I was thinking of gunpowder—a fort—things like that," Fritz said.

"Wait—I have the best idea," said Francis. "We could dig pits, and have tigers in them—and when the pirates fall in they'll get et!"

Only Johann took him seriously. "I don't know about the tigers, but a few pits might be a good idea," he said. "But first we must get rid of that ship. We don't want the pirates to find us before we're ready."

There wasn't much left on the ship besides some barrels of gunpowder. Johann and the older boys unloaded the ship quickly. Then they lit a fuse and rowed toward shore. They waited for what seemed like a very long time.

"Do you think something's gone wrong with the fuse?" asked Ernst.

Johann frowned as he steered the raft. "Well, we're certainly not going back to find out."

A moment later the entire ship exploded. Masts, spars, and timbers flew into the air. On the beach, Francis hopped up and down with excitement. "KaBOOM!" he shouted at the top of his voice. "KaBOOM!"

The Robinsons hauled their guns and gunpowder to the clifftop that overlooked their beach. To the rear of the cliff, the land sloped back down to the jungle. "We'll build a fort up here," said Johann. "It's easier to hold off an enemy when he's below you. The pirates are sure to go around the cliff and try to reach us from the side or rear. So we'll put our tree snares and pits just off the beach—"

"And the tigers," added Francis.

"That's your job, Francis," teased Ernst. "Don't forget—you're in charge of the tigers."

They all began working right away to set things up. Using coconut shells, gunpowder, and a fuse sealed with candlewax, Fritz invented a bomb. Ernst and Roberta helped him make a good supply. The job took hours. They had lots of time to talk, and shared their hopes and dreams.

"The thing about me," Ernst said, "is I'd like to *be* something in the world, and I like to read. That's why I'd like to go to school."

"You ought to go to school in London," Roberta said. "There are parties and dances, men in high hats—did you ever wear a high hat?"

Ernst shook his head.

"Oh, I'd love to see you in one," said Roberta. "You'd be handsome!" She was quiet for a long time and then said, half to herself, "There must be something my grandfather could do."

"Well, I doubt if *I'll* ever go to London," Fritz said. "That's not for me—high hats and wearing shoes every day—"

Just then Francis walked up, carrying a string of bells. "What's this?" asked Roberta. "A pirate alarm?"

Francis nodded so seriously that Fritz and Ernst howled with laughter. But Roberta made them stop. "What about your tiger—have you caught him yet?" she asked.

"I can't until Fritz digs the pit," Francis answered. "Otherwise I won't have any place to keep him!"

"All right, Francis," said Fritz, wearily picking up a shovel. "We'll get ready for your tiger right now."

After days of working from dawn to dusk, everyone's temper grew short. Ernst and Fritz had a silly fight over a little piece of rope. "Maybe I've been pushing you all too hard," Johann said. "We need to relax for a change." He thought a minute. "I know—tomorrow will be the first national holiday in the history of this island! We'll have a race—and lots more!"

That night after dinner, Roberta and the boys made banners from the ship's old signal flags. Then they twisted flowers into colorful chains. They were almost finished when the dogs began to growl.

"What is it now?" asked Johann. He went out on the porch and peered over the railing, but saw nothing. "Oh, just be quiet, both of you," he said crossly. Like everyone else he was nervous and tired.

Suddenly the whole clearing echoed with howls and hisses.

"I bet that's my tiger," yelled Francis.

"Everyone stay upstairs until I have a look," Johann ordered. "Fritz, you come with me."

Taking the dogs and a torch, they went to the shadowy pit that Fritz had dug. Carefully, they looked in. A huge snarling animal clawed at the sides, unable to leap out. "Well, Francis got his tiger," Fritz said with a grin. He and his father put palm fronds over the pit. "But let's not cover him too well, Father—we might forget where he is and fall in!"

Next morning the flags and flower chains gave the place a special holiday look. The first event of the day was the race. The racers were Francis on his elephant, Roberta riding the zebra, Ernst on the ostrich, and Fritz aboard the donkey they had rescued from the ship. Johann was the timekeeper and referee, and Elizabeth held the starting gun. They sat to one side, with a cake on a table in front of them.

At a signal from Elizabeth, Johann stood up and began a speech. "Now remember, la—dies and gen—tle—men . . . the course goes from the animal pens to the beach. You go around it twice. And to the winnah—this wonderful cu—li—nary creation—which all of us will eat!"

Everyone began giggling.

"And serving as our starter todaaaayyyy," Johann went on, quite carried away, "is this looovely laaadddy. . . ."

By now the riders were laughing so hard that they couldn't keep their animals in line.

"Quick!" Johann said to Elizabeth. She braced herself, pointed the gun to the sky, and squeezed the trigger. Almost at once the donkey and ostrich ran into each other. The elephant made for the jungle. The air was full of cries of "Not *that* way, you stupid bird!" and "Whoa!" and "No fair walking, you have to *ride*!"

The race was only half over when Roberta came running back from the beach. "Pirates offshore!" she gasped. "A ship and two long-boats!"

"Everyone to your stations right away!" Johann shouted. "Remember your orders!"

"I'll get the guns!" "Come with me!" "Over here!" "Watch out!" Amid all the noise, the race animals fled into the jungle. The tiger growled in his pit. "Shh!" said Francis as he ran past. He stopped to look in.

"Not now, Francis—come on!" screamed Elizabeth, dragging him away by his collar.

By the time everyone got to the hilltop fort, a group of pirates were already on the beach. The wild-looking men moved forward into the jungle. A few were trapped in Ernst's tree snares, but the rest reached the bridge in the clearing. "Quick, Ernst!" called Fritz. They pulled on long ropes that had been covered with dirt. Below, the bridge suddenly fell apart, sending several men into the stream.

Fritz yelled with delight, but the pirates forded the stream and kept coming. They crossed in front of the animal pens and headed for the hill.

"They're right in line with the pit!" said Roberta.

Everyone looked down. Fritz had to clamp his hand over Francis's mouth to keep him from cheering. "Over this way," Ernst whispered. "A little more to your left. . . ."

The next moment there were terrified screams and wild snarling as three pirates fell into the tiger pit. Francis squirmed away from Fritz and began yelling. "He got 'em! My tiger got 'em!" With a gasp Elizabeth covered her eyes. But all three men managed to climb out on logs thrown down by their friends. They fled toward the boat, limping. Their bloody clothes were cut to ribbons. The tiger climbed out, too, and ran for the jungle.

Now some pirates were climbing the hill. Ernst tugged at another long rope. "Help!" he gasped. "It's too hard!" Fritz leaned over the edge of the fort's log wall and helped him pull. This time several pre-aimed crossbows fired. But the pirates kept climbing.

Suddenly a jangling noise came from the other side of the hill. "My pirate alarm!" cried Francis. "They're coming up the other side!"

The Robinsons rushed across and found a second group of pirates on the hillside. Their leader was the same man that Fritz and Ernst had knocked out when they rescued Roberta. He stopped climbing and held up a white flag. "We only want the boy," he called. "Give him to us and we'll leave you alone."

"Put away that flag and come get him!" yelled Johann. "We're ready!" He gave the signal, and the whole family began tossing coconut bombs on both groups of pirates.

"Did you see that one?" yelled Ernst.

"Watch this one!" cried Fritz.

But not even the bombs could stop all the pirates. The family became terrified as the pirates climbed higher and higher.

Then over the bomb explosions came a deeper noise, the booming of distant cannons. The pirates stopped climbing at once and fled down to their longboats.

"Are they trying to shell us from the ship?" asked Roberta as the booming continued.

"No, they must've mixed up their signals," said Elizabeth. Puzzled, she lifted the telescope and searched the horizon. "A merchant ship!" she cried. "It's firing on the pirates!" She handed the telescope to Johann.

"Roberta—you look," he said. "Do you recognize it?"

"It's one of my grandfather's ships!" she shouted. "I told you he would come!"

Suddenly there came a terrific BOOM, and the pirate ship blew to bits. This time even Elizabeth cheered. Then everyone ran to the beach to welcome Roberta's grandfather.

Several days later, the Robinsons sat down to a farewell tea with Roberta and Captain Smith. Ernst was so excited he could hardly eat or drink. He and Fritz were to sail to London, too. "I always wanted to go to school," he kept saying. "But I never dreamed I'd go to the university. Thank you again," he said to Roberta's grandfather.

"Don't thank *me,* my boy! I'm sure you'll do well, and you certainly deserve it." Captain Smith drained his cup. "As for the rest of you," he said, "Are you sure you wouldn't like to go back to Europe? Or shall I send a ship to take you to New Guinea?"

Johann looked at Elizabeth. She put her hand on his shoulder. "Now that we have to decide, I think my husband and I would rather just stay here."

Amazed and delighted, Johann flung his arms around his wife. "Are you sure it's what *you* want?" he asked.

Elizabeth nodded. "As long as Ernst and Fritz can go, I'm happy," she said. "It's been a good life here."

Suddenly it all hit Francis. "You mean *I* don't have to go?"

Johann smiled and shook his head. "We'll keep you with us for a few more years."

"Hurray!" yelled Francis. "I won't have to leave my animals!" He ran down the stairs to tell them.

Fritz followed him down. He wanted to say good-by to the zebra. He tried to run but his stiff leather shoes were hurting his feet. He wasn't so sure he wanted to go to London.

After tea everyone walked to the beach, where the Captain's longboat was waiting. Everyone who was going climbed in. "Of course you realize there'll be more people settling on this island," said the Captain. "So you won't be without neighbors after a while."

Johann and Elizabeth nodded. That didn't seem like a bad idea.

Suddenly Fritz began to untie his shoes. "Not for me—I'm not going!" he yelled loudly. To everyone's surprise he pulled off shoes, jacket, and tie. He handed them to Ernst. "Here's some extras, little brother," he said. "Good luck in the world!"

Then, barefoot and happy, he jumped out of the longboat and ran to join Francis and his parents. Together they waved at Ernst and the others until they disappeared from view.

Backpacking—The Easy Way

IF YOU'VE NEVER SLIPPED A PACK on your back and headed for the woods, you're missing out on some lively adventure. So now is the time to get started.

As a beginning backpacker, don't just take off all by yourself. Bring along a guide. A 15- or 16-year-old boy or girl who knows the outdoors would be fine. You may also want two or three friends your own age to come along. That way you can all share in the fun.

How long should your hike be? Make the first one short. Save overnight hikes for later, when you have more experience. To start, a 45-minute walk with a pack on your back should be plenty. In that amount of time, you can hike about a mile—unless you stop to look at leaves or birds or footprints. Then you won't walk as far. If you add time for a long lunch and 45 minutes for your return trip, the whole outing should take about three or four hours.

The first thing to know before you pack up is what gear you'll need—flashlight, canteen, compass, Band-Aids, and such. The Day Hike Checklist on page 41 will save you time figuring this out. Don't pack too much. Extra weight

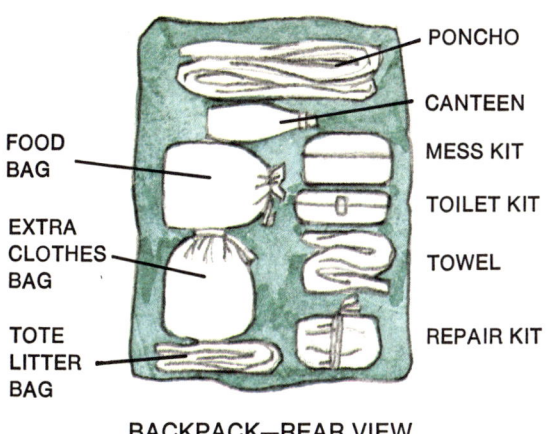
BACKPACK—REAR VIEW

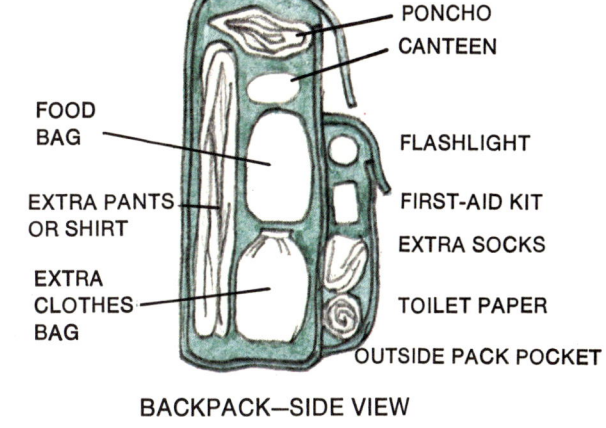
BACKPACK—SIDE VIEW

can tire you out. When you load up for a short hike, the pack should be no more than one-fourth your weight. And it can easily be kept to one-fifth your weight. So if you weigh 80 pounds, your pack should weigh no more than 16 to 20 pounds.

When you're packing, don't put all of the heavy gear at the bottom. A bottom-heavy pack doesn't "ride" comfortably on your back. Neither does one that's overloaded on either side. Also, be sure that a cup handle or flashlight isn't in a spot where it will poke you in the back. And pad the side of the pack that's toward your back with your extra pants and shirt.

A proper pack is a large sack full of smaller sacks. The weight is evenly spread out. Everything has its own place. A rain poncho, for instance, should be at the top of your pack—even on a sunny day. Then the poncho will be handy in case a rainstorm sneaks up on you. If you bury the poncho deep down inside, you'll end up pulling your pack apart when the rain starts.

One of the best ways to store

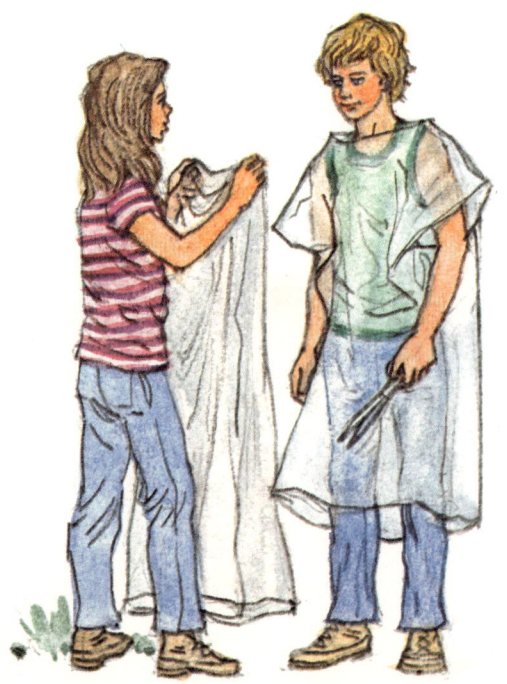

For a lightweight poncho, use a plastic garbage bag. All you do is cut three holes —one for your head and one for each arm.

pieces of gear is in plastic bags. They are easy to get and come in many sizes. Besides, plastic bags are waterproof. And you can see what is in them. Opening and closing them is easy because they tie with a twist-tab.

What's the best backpack for you? If you're five feet tall or less, a giant bag 25" (inches) high by 14" wide by 10" deep would be too big for you. It might be half your size! On the other hand, a bag 12" by 11" by 5" would hardly give you the space you need even for a day hike. So find a pack about midway between those sizes. It should have room for your day-hike gear and some extra room as well. Someday you might want to use your backpack for overnight hikes. Then you'll be carrying a sleeping bag and a tent in the pack.

A good backpack should be made of tough, waterproof material such as heavy-duty nylon. The pack should have lots of pocket space around the outside.

When you go backpacking, your feet do a lot of hard work. So be kind to them. Before you leave on your hike, trim your toenails. Then wash your feet and dust them with foot powder. To stop blisters, rub some soap along your heels. Soap keeps your heels from rubbing hard against the backs of your shoes.

Wear lightweight socks—nylon, cotton, or wool—underneath a pair of heavy ones, preferably wool. The heavy ones will pad your feet. So wear them even in warm weather. Make sure the socks fit well and have no rough seams or darned places. Then slip your feet into a pair of comfortable, broken-in leather-top shoes. Ankle-high shoes are best. They give your ankles extra support if you step on a stone or in a rut. If you don't have ankle-high shoes, wear whatever you've got. But leather soles are slippery on rocks and in wet places. So rubber or cord soles are better for you.

Before you leave for your hike, give your parents some information. What patch of woods are you headed for? When will you be back? Who is your guide? Which of your friends are going along?

If you come to a highway along your route, walk in a single file. Your guide should lead the way. Walk on the left side of the road, facing traffic. Maybe for some good reason (It had better be good!) you'll be delayed, and won't get back until dark. If so, each person in your group should wrap a white handkerchief around his or her right leg. Then car drivers will be able to see you more easily. Also use your flashlights. Beam them down on the road; not into the drivers' faces.

What's for lunch when you get where you're going? Since you're covering only about two miles, a couple of sandwiches and a thermos of juice should be enough. For a snack along the way, you might enjoy an apple or a candy bar.

Later, maybe on your second hike, you'll want to do your own cooking. Then you can bring along an aluminum-foil-wrapped lunch that you've put together at home. In it you might put a raw hamburger, a raw potato cut in quarters, some onion slices, some carrots cut in half lengthwise, and a chunk of butter or margarine. When you get to your campsite, ask your guide to help you build a small fire. Then toss your foil-wrapped meat and vegetables into the embers for about ten minutes on each side. What a super meal! You don't need much cooking gear, and cleanup's a snap.

When you're ready to head for home, soak down your fire until it's out cold. Then stir the soaked ashes with a stick. Drench them again for good measure. After that, crumple up your used foil. Carry it away with you in your own plastic litter bag. Do that, and you'll live up to the backpacker's code: *Take with you only what you need. Leave behind only your footsteps.*

Day Hike Checklist

Items in red are a must for any day hike. Also bring items with a * if you do aluminum-foil cooking.

WEAR (or carry in top of pack)

    Sweater or **jacket**
    Rainhat or **hood**
    Poncho or **raincoat**
    Rubbers, lightweight

CARRY IN CLOTHING POCKETS

    White handkerchief
    Wallet and **money** *(include change for phone call)*
    Toilet paper in plastic bag
    Two or three Band-Aids
    Compass

CARRY IN TOP OR OUTSIDE POCKETS OF PACK

    First-aid kit containing:
      insect repellent
      roll bandage
      small scissors
      tweezers or **needles**
      (for removing splinters)
      tape
      burn ointment
      snake-bite kit
    Canteen or **thermos**
    Extra pair of socks
    (in case your feet get wet)
    Flashlight
    *Mess kit containing:
      knife, spoon, fork
      deep-sided plate
      cup

CARRY INSIDE PACK

    Food bag
    Tote litter bag

Plastic or **cloth clothesbag containing:**
    extra shirt
    extra pants
    extra handkerchief
    extra socks
   *gardener's gloves *(for hot objects)*
Sneakers
Toilet kit containing:
   washcloth
   soap
   comb
   hand mirror
Towel
Repair kit containing:
   rubber bands
   safety pins
   shoelaces
   cord
   extra plastic bags
  *fire starter *(milk carton strips)*
*Paper towels

HAVE GUIDE CARRY

    Jackknife
    Matches (wooden) in waterproof case

YOU MIGHT ALSO BRING

    Watch
    Camera, film
    Map
    Dark glasses
    Notebook, pencil
    Binoculars
    Rope
    String
    Nature books

Big Bird

Have you ever seen a bird that is taller than a grown person? You may have—if you've ever seen an ostrich. The ostrich is the biggest bird in the world. A large male may be 8 feet (more than 2 meters) tall. It may weigh more than 300 pounds (135 kilograms). A hen, or female, ostrich is just a little smaller.

Naturally, a bird that big lays a very large egg. In fact, the ostrich egg is the biggest of all bird eggs. It can be 6 to 8 inches (15 to 20 centimeters) long and weigh up to 3 pounds (well over a kilogram). One egg can make an omelet for 12 people!

Not only is the ostrich big, but it is funny looking—for a bird.

Ostriches have long, featherless legs and necks. Some ostriches have blue skin on these parts. Others have pink skin. Ostrich heads are small with big, sharp beaks. Their large eyes have thick, black lashes.

Unlike most birds, ostriches cannot fly. They are too big, and their wings are too small. But ostriches do very well without flying. They can run very fast on their long, strong legs—up to 40 miles (64 kilometers) an hour. And it's a good thing! There are many predators—hungry enemies—in the area of Africa where ostriches live. Lions and jackals and hyenas would all love a fine meal of ostrich meat.

Fortunately, an ostrich is able to protect itself in many ways. Because it has a long neck and long legs, it can see far across the land and spot the approach of danger. If it cannot get away by running, it can use its strong legs and sharp beak as weapons.

Another fine protection that the ostrich has is camouflage. People used to think that the ostrich buried its head in the sand to hide itself. But the ostrich is too smart a bird for that! What the bird does is hide by making itself hard to see. If the ostrich is sitting on its eggs, it won't run. Instead, it will put its head down and stretch its long neck out against the ground. In this position it looks more like a desert rock or a clump of thorny bushes than an ostrich. As long as it does not move, a predator probably won't recognize it.

But there is more to ostrich life than protection. Nests must be built and babies raised. The male ostrich usually makes the nest. He digs a hole in the sand. Then he invites a number of hens to mate with him. He attracts them with a courting dance. He runs about and flaps his wings at them. His wings and tail have beautiful black-and-white plumes that flutter as he jumps up and down. By dancing, he also tries to chase away other males. If they won't go, there is a fight.

When the birds have mated, the hens begin to lay eggs in the nest. Often there are more than 20 eggs in one nest. Although they may be laid by several different hens, the oldest—the top hen—lays the most. She chases the younger hens around and won't let them sit on the nest. She sits there most of the day. In the afternoon she leaves the nest to look for food, and the male ostrich takes over. He sits on the eggs all through the night.

An ostrich egg takes from 5 to 6 weeks to hatch. But long before that, the chicks can be heard peeping inside the shell. The mother and father ostriches put their heads down by the eggs and peep back. So while the babies are still inside the eggs, they learn to know their parents' voices.

A baby ostrich is 1 foot (30 centimeters) tall at hatching. It grows another foot (30 centimeters) each month. By the time it is 5 months old, it is 5 feet (150 centimeters) tall and can run almost as fast as its parents.

When the eggs have all hatched and the babies are able to run about, the parent birds lead them away from the nest to look for food.

The babies peck at everything they see on the ground. They have to learn what is good to eat and what is not. Ostriches will eat almost anything. They like seeds, fruit, and flowers. They like insects and lizards. Sometimes they even eat stones. A few stones are good for them. The stones stay in their stomachs and help digestion by grinding up food.

The most dangerous time for ostriches is when they are very small. Then their only defense is to lie still and hope that a predator does not find them. When a dangerous animal is sighted, the father ostrich makes a deep booming sound. He cries, "Boo-boo!" and the babies hide. The parents have many other peeps and pipings to tell the chicks when to lie still and when it is safe to move again. The adult birds also have tricks to lure a predator away. They pretend to have a broken leg or wing, and they flop around on the ground. Most lions know about this and ignore the big birds. They keep on searching for the helpless babies. If the enemy animal gets too close to the chicks, the father may launch an attack. He stretches out his long neck and hisses. He flaps his plumes. He may even deliver a well-placed kick, which can send the predator flying into a thorn bush.

Before the chicks are hatched, the ostrich flocks are small. There may be only 5 or 6 birds in one group. But later, a family made up of about 5 adults and 20 chicks joins with other ostrich groups. Then a flock may number 50 to 100 birds—or even more. Sometimes ostriches stay with herds of antelopes, zebras, or gnus that move about the great plains. Ostriches like to search for food with these animals. The herds scare insects up from the grass as they walk. When a fat grasshopper flies up beside a zebra or a gnu, the ostrich is right there to grab it.

The ostriches are also helpful to the other animals because the ostriches can see so far away. When an ostrich sees a sign of danger and starts to run, the other animals know that they should run, too.

Ostriches can live for 50 to 70 years. But although they lay many eggs and protect their babies well, they are dying out in the wild. Long ago, their ancestors lived in southern Europe and in Asia. Now ostriches are found only in the wildest parts of Africa and in national parks. Because people need more and more land to raise food, the ostriches have been pushed farther and farther back into the desert regions. During World War II, some Arabs ate the last Arabian ostrich! Perhaps in time all these remarkable birds will be killed. Perhaps there will only be a few left in zoos.

But some may also remain on ostrich farms. Such farms were started as long ago as 1860. Ostrich feathers were highly prized by hat designers, and ostrich skins make soft leather. So ostrich farms have been successful businesses. The birds are easily tamed and have been taught to carry loads and pull carts. And, as you read in *Swiss Family Robinson,* ostriches have even been used for riding! But the owner must never forget those strong legs and that sharp beak. If an ostrich does not like you, it can do a lot of damage!

Mickey and Goofy On a Wilderness Trek

MICKEY AND GOOFY were off on what they hoped would be a glorious two-week camping trip in Yukkapuk National Park. But somewhere near Geezer Geyser, they had turned off the trail to take a picture of a moose. And now they were lost!

"We need a compass," Mickey said. "Did you bring one?"

"Yup!" Goofy beamed. "Right here in my sat-nap . . . my nap-sap . . . I mean, my knapsack!" Goofy opened his pack and pulled out a compass. Unfortunately, it was the kind of compass that's used for drawing circles.

"That's not exactly the kind of compass I had in mind," Mickey said. "I meant a compass that shows north, east, south, and west."

Mickey sat down on a rock. "Now we're REALLY lost!"

"I think I once heard that moss grows on the north side of a tree," Goofy said, trying to be helpful. "Let's walk around that tree and see if we can find any moss."

"There's moss growing all around this tree," Mickey noted.

"So what do we do now?" Goofy asked.

Just then, a funny little woman with frizzy green hair and bright, twinkling eyes stepped out from behind the tree.

"Can I help you?" she asked with a smile. "I'm a wood nymph. I know all about the woods."

"We're lost," Mickey said. "Can you help us find our way?"

"Of course!" the wood nymph replied. "But it will cost you a quarter!"

"Fair enough," Mickey said, dropping a twenty-five-cent piece into her hand. "I guess wood nymphs have to live, too!"

"Thank you," said the wood nymph, pocketing the quarter.

"Just keep going in that direction," the nymph said, pointing, "until you come to a fork in the road. Then bear right."

"We've already come to a fork in the road," said Goofy, picking up a plastic fork some picnicker had dropped.

"She doesn't mean THAT kind of fork," Mickey said.

Gathering up their knapsacks, Mickey and Goofy thanked the wood nymph and trekked off.

"I thought you said you knew your way around the forest," said Goofy, as they zigzagged through the endless number of trees.

"I know my way AROUND it!" Mickey said. "I just don't know my way THROUGH it!"

Two hours and 43,645 trees later, they came to the fork in the road, and went to the right. Soon they came to the edge of what looked like a wide, deep river.

"How will we ever get across that river?" Goofy exclaimed.

"I can row you across," said a small, familiar voice. "For twenty-five cents each!" There, just below the riverbank, was the funny little woman with the frizzy green hair, sitting in a rowboat.

"Boy! You sure get around!" Mickey said. He dug down deep in his pocket and finally produced fifty cents.

"All aboard!" said the nymph. "Don't stand up in the boat. This is a very deep and treacherous river!"

"Oh-oh!" said Mickey as they reached the far side of the river. "We left our sap-naps . . . I mean, knapsacks, on the other side.

"I'll get them for you," the nymph said. She stepped right into the water and waded to the other side. There she picked up the knapsacks and waded back to Mickey and Goofy. The water just barely splashed over the toes of her hiking boots.

"That'll be twenty-five cents, please!"

"I thought you said the river was deep and treacherous!" said Mickey, handing her another quarter. "You just waded right through it!"

"It *is* deep and treacherous... during the spring floods."

Mickey and Goofy waved farewell to the wood nymph and started off again.

"I wonder how that nymph got to the river before we did." Mickey sounded puzzled.

"Maybe she took a taxi," said Goofy, trying to be funny. But Mickey was too tired to laugh.

Hour after hour went by. The sun was sinking slowly in the western sky by the time they came to a sign that said "BEAR LEFT." They immediately turned left. Suddenly they stood face to face with the biggest bear they had ever seen.

"GRRRRRRR!" roared the bear, looking very unfriendly.

Goofy and Mickey made a dash for the nearest tree!

They scrambled up the tree and climbed out on a limb. Below, the bear growled and bared his long, white teeth.

"Now what do we do?" Goofy said.

"Do you want the bear to go away?"

There was that familiar voice again. This time it came from inside the tree. A frizzy green head popped out of a large knothole in the tree trunk.

"Twenty-five cents, please!"

"You!" Mickey said, almost falling off the limb in astonishment! "How did you—"

"GRRRAAARRRRR!" growled the bear, starting up the tree.

"Better pay her, Mickey!" Goofy advised.

Mickey dropped two dimes and a nickel into the wood nymph's hand.

"GO AWAY, BEAR!" the nymph commanded.

53

The bear immediately stopped growling, pulled in its claws and wandered off.

From high in the tree, Mickey and Goofy could see the whole countryside. They discovered that they were nearly out of the woods.

"You know, before we leave these woods, there's just one thing I want to know," Mickey said to the wood nymph. "How do you manage to get around so fast?"

The nymph pulled a telephone out of the tree. "Operator," she said, "please give me Forest-Tree, Tree-Tree, Fir-Tree!"

Suddenly, hundreds of telephones rang out. And from every tree and from behind every rock appeared a funny little woman with frizzy green hair!

"It's a family business," explained the nymph.

"That'll be twenty-five cents, please!" said a hundred small voices.

Malay Pirates

Imagine a man with a great dark beard and mustache. He is standing proudly on a sailing ship. And he is ordering some poor fellow to walk the plank. This fierce man is dressed in a brocaded coat and trousers tucked into high boots. He wears a gold hoop earring and a large hat. And, of course, he carries a sword and pistol.

Who is this man? He is most people's idea of a pirate. He is what you think of when you hear the famous pirate names Blackbeard, Black Bart, and Captain Kidd. But many pirates looked nothing like this picture.

In fact, most pirates were not at all dashing and dramatic. Rather, they were poor and drunken. They dressed in rags. They spent their loot foolishly. They lived very short lives. And not all of them were men.

A pirate is a man or woman who commits armed robbery on the high seas or robs on land from ships. Piracy has been practiced for thousands of years. In Greece long ago it was even thought an honorable profession. And piracy has been found all over the world. The most famous pirates were born in America, Europe, and North Africa. But for centuries, native-born pirates also thrived in and around the Malay Peninsula and Borneo in Southeast Asia. Look at the map on this page to get a good idea of where that is. The Robinsons of *Swiss Family Robinson* were stranded somewhere in that area.

Who were the Southeast Asian

pirates? Some were Malays. They are a short, brown-skinned people who live on the Malay Peninsula and in Indonesia and the Philippines. Other pirates came from the North Borneo coast. Pirates have a reputation for being villainous and cold-blooded. And these were certainly no exception. They thought nothing of killing people they captured at sea or of sending them into slavery. And to get more slaves, they raided villages every year and kidnapped thousands of people.

While piracy had always been popular around the Malay Peninsula, it became more so at the beginning of the 1800s. This was because Europeans came there to get pepper and other spices. Many of the Malays who were sea traders found their trade taken over by the Europeans.

In order to make a living, a lot of Malays became pirates. They robbed other local traders. And once a trader lost all he had, he too might join the ranks of the pirates. In this way, the numbers of Malay pirates grew and grew.

Malay pirates attacked European trading ships as well, even though these ships were heavily armed. Sometimes a European boat was wrecked or stuck without a wind to fill its sails and make it move. Then it might find itself surrounded by a fleet of pirate ships. Imagine this: Hundreds of Malay pirates are standing on the narrow decks of their boats. They are dressed in bright red coats and decorated with feathers. Or else they are barechested, wearing turbans. They beat gongs, shriek, and dance before their attack.

Although the European sailors

had many, many guns, the Malays often overpowered them. Why? Because there was such a great number of Malay pirates.

The Malay area was a perfect place for pirates. Its many rivers, creeks, and channels made excellent hideaways. These could be used for an attack—or a quick escape. The pirates also were helped by local rulers who backed them in their work. The rulers gave the pirates guns and gunpowder. In return, the pirates gave these chiefs part of their loot. And because the pirates were backed by royalty, piracy was considered an honorable job.

By the 1820s, acts of piracy took place so often that trade around the peninsula almost stopped. The British government, which wanted to trade there, didn't know what to do.

But then an unlikely heroine saved the day. She was *Diana*—a steamboat named *Diana,* that is. The steamboat, a fairly recent invention, was sent in by the East India Company, which controlled the Malay trade.

The pirates' ships were sailing ships, and so they depended on the wind to move. But the *Diana* did not have to wait for favorable winds. Spouting black steam, the *Diana* overtook the pirates' boats. And the pirates were captured. In a few years, this churning, mechanical monster had helped reduce piracy around the Malay peninsula.

However, that solved only part of the problem. For the most daring pirates came from northwest Borneo. This area today is known as East Malaysia. These pirates were highly skilled sailors—and vicious killers. They could call on thousands of men and hundreds of light boats to help them in an attack. These pirates controlled trade along the northwest Borneo coast and in the large rivers.

That is, they did until they ran into an Englishman named James Brooke. Brooke decided to rid the area of pirates. And with a British navy captain named Harry Keppel, he managed to ambush the Borneo pirates in 1849. Many of the pirates were killed and thousands left their boats and ran away.

Then Brooke got the British Royal Navy to clean up the area of two other pirate groups. So by 1879 not much piracy was going on in the area. In fact, by then, not much of it was going on anywhere. However, sea piracy has never disappeared completely. And today the world has yet another kind of pirate to deal with—the air pirate, or highjacker. But that's another story. . . .

Getting "Unlost"

GETTING LOST is the easiest thing in the world to do. That's why most people are so good at it. But losing your way can be scary, especially if you're in the woods.

Luckily, Mother Nature can be a big help to you in getting "unlost." The earth's shadows can lead you to where you want to go. And —believe it or not—so can some plants. The stars and the sun also give direction signs that you can use to find your way.

Before you can make use of the sun, you have to know a few facts. The earth spins like a fat top. Each spin takes 24 hours, one day. When your part of the earth turns toward the sun, you see the sun rise in the east. When your part turns away from the sun, you see the sun go down in the west.

Let's get a bit more practical. Early some morning, go outside to see the sunrise. Glance at the sun. (Don't stare! It will injure your eyes.) You'll know you're looking east. What's the opposite of east? West is. That means west is behind your back. From here on, finding north and south is a cinch. When you face the east, north is on your left, south on your right.

Now, look at what's around you. Suppose your house is right in front of you. Then it's east of you. Where is your school? To your right? Then it's south of you. Since it's also to the right of your house, it's south of your house, too. Because you move around, your school won't always be south of you. But it will always be south of your house. How about that patch of woods you like to wander around in? If that's behind you, it's west of you. It's also west of your house. That's important to remember. If you enter those woods by going west, you can get home by heading in the opposite direction— east.

Another time you may make use of the sunrise is when you take a hike early on a bright morning. If the sun's over your right shoulder, you'll know you're heading north. If the sun's over your left shoulder, you're heading south.

You can also find your directions when the sun is setting in the west. Face the sun. Since that's west, east is behind you. North is on your right. South is on your left.

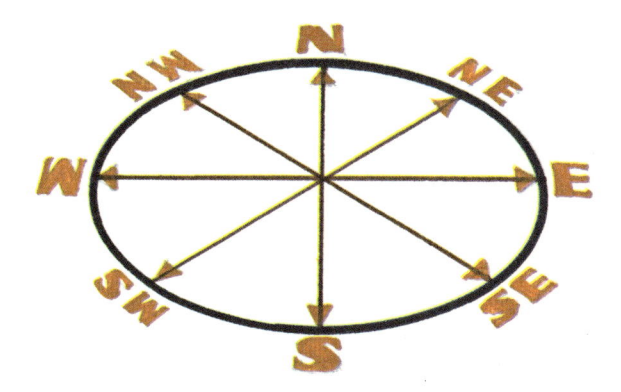

One thing more. When something isn't directly north (N) or east (E) of you, but midway between those two points, we say it's northeast (NE). If it's between south (S) and west (W), it's southwest (SW). In all, there are eight main directions you should learn— N, NE, E, SE, S, SW, W, NW.

Now you know how to find your direction at sunrise or sunset. But how do you find your way during the day when the sun is hanging somewhere else in the sky?

With a friend or two, take a short walk into the woods some sunny day. When you get to an open space, look up to see if you can spot the sun. Find yourself a straight, dead branch about a foot long. Push it into the ground so that it *doesn't* cast a shadow. That means you must point it directly at the sun. Within 15 or 20 minutes, a shadow will start creeping out from the base of the stick. This shadow will form a pretty accurate west-east line.

West is *at the stick* and east *at the shadow tip*. This is an old woodsman's trick for getting "unlost."

Since you're already out in the woods, you might as well do some snooping. You've probably heard that moss grows on the north side of trees, especially in damp spots. It does. But it also grows on all the other sides. So forget about following it. You're likely to end up getting dizzy.

However, there are plants that *can* help you find your direction. You have probably seen goldenrod, with its bright yellow flowers growing in clusters at the top of the stem. When goldenrod blooms in the summer and autumn, the flower clusters always lean to the north. If

GOLDENROD

BARREL CACTUS

you live in the Southwest, you may find a plant called a barrel cactus. It, too, always leans toward the north. Both of these plants can help you get "unlost."

At night there's no better friend to show you the way than the North Star. To find it, you'll need help from the Big Dipper. The Big Dipper is a group of seven stars formed in the shape of a dipper, or long-handled cup. When you locate the Big Dipper, look for the two stars farthest from its handle. Draw an imaginary line between them. One end of the line will point toward a very bright star. That's the North Star. Notice that it's also at the *end* of the handle of a smaller dipper. This dipper is called (you guessed it) the Little Dipper. It, too, has seven stars.

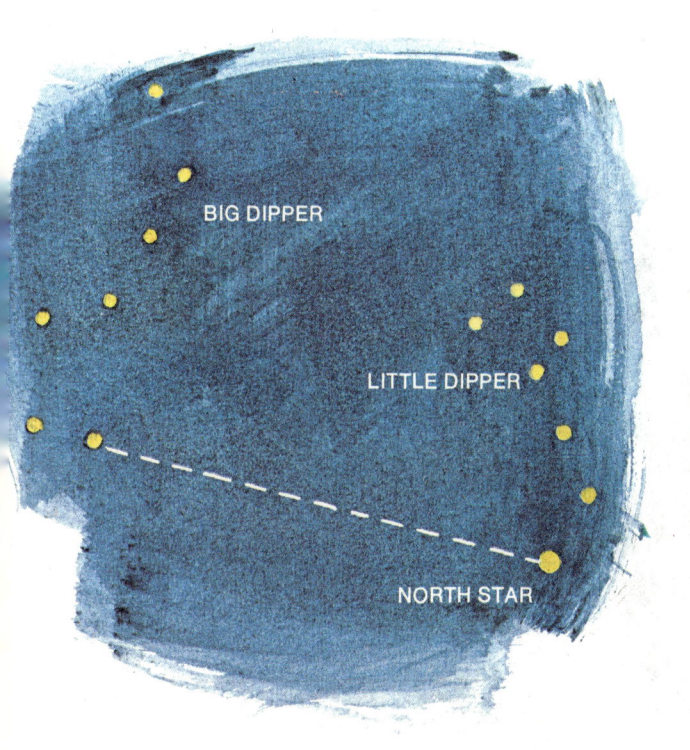

Mother Nature is a big help in getting "unlost." But your best bet is to use a compass. For 50 cents or so you can get a small one. It will have a swinging needle and a "face" showing the eight main directions. Using the compass is simple. One end of the needle (which is marked) always points north. The other end always points south. All you have to do is line up the needle so that the north end points to the N on the compass face. If you keep your compass needle steady, you'll be able to follow a path heading in any direction you choose. So you see, getting "unlost" can be almost as easy as getting lost!

DATE DUE

Mr 16 '86